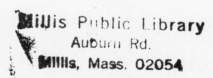

P9-AQT-713

THE SOLDIER THROUGH THE AGES

THE BRITISH
REDCOAT
OF THE NAPOLEONIC WARS

Martin Windrow

Illustrated by

Angus McBride

Franklin Watts
New York   London   Toronto   Sydney

© Franklin Watts Limited 1985

First published in Great Britain in 1985 by
Franklin Watts Ltd
12a Golden Square
London W1

First published in the USA by
Franklin Watts Inc.
387 Park Avenue South
New York
N.Y. 10016

First published in Australia by
Franklin Watts Australia
1 Campbell Street
Artarmon
NSW 2064

UK edition ISBN: 0 86313 297 9
US edition ISBN: 0-531-10082-0
Library of Congress Catalog Card
No: 85-50763

Designed by James Marks

Printed in Belgium

Contents

The recruiting sergeant's promises

From 1799 to 1815 Europe was ravaged by the Napoleonic Wars between France, led by the brilliant soldier-emperor Napoleon Bonaparte, and shifting alliances of other nations. Napoleon's dashing young generals and huge armies of veterans occupied or beat into submission most of the continent, except for Britain. Britain was saved by the difficulty of invading across the English Channel and by her powerful Royal Navy. But for most of this period her small, rather old-fashioned army was too weak to fight Napoleon's armies on land on any large scale.

From the earliest years of these wars the Royal Navy, led by skilled admirals such as Lord Nelson, the victor of Trafalgar in 1805, won a series of sea battles against the French. British warships protected British merchant fleets all over the world, and trade kept Britain rich. The fleets that protected and enriched the country were always well manned: in coastal areas press-gangs of sailors were literally allowed to kidnap likely men for service at sea. But recruits for the army had to be found – often with difficulty – from among volunteers.

If the navy had prestige, the army was despised. The "redcoats" – nicknamed after the uniform color adopted as far back as the 1640s – had won few victories in the past thirty years. In the days before the raising of a civilian police force, troops were sometimes used to put down riots, which did not increase their popularity. They had such a bad reputation for drunkenness and violence that enlistment was considered only a little less disgraceful than a life of crime. Indeed, recruiting officers took convicted men straight from the courtroom, for army service instead of prison.

▷ To the music of fife and drum, and plenty of free ale, farm workers listen to a recruiting sergeant's expansive promises outside an English ale house in about 1800. Each regiment sent out parties of picked men, their smartest uniforms tricked out with ribbons, to "beat up for volunteers" in the surrounding villages. They offered bored, sometimes penniless young men a life of travel, adventure and glory if they signed on for seven years. The unpleasant side of army life was never mentioned! They also offered the volunteer a large cash bounty. But when he woke up next morning, with a headache from drinking the King's health, he was lucky if he still had a few coins in his pocket.

So it is all the more impressive that between 1803 and 1815 generals like Sir John Moore and the Duke of Wellington made such improvements that the redcoat became respected throughout Europe. The secret was common sense and decent treatment. Sir John taught his men to be better soldiers by example and praise, rather than by fear of the whip. Wellington took the trouble to learn just what his men could be expected to accomplish. In 1815 it was the redcoat, with his German, Dutch and Belgian allies, who finally defeated Napoleon at the battle of Waterloo.

Battalion drill

The new recruit was marched to the head-quarters of his regiment – the depot. He was assigned a barrack room and issued with his clothing and gear. He soon began to learn about his strange new life.

Each regiment was usually divided into two battalions, anything from 400 to 800 men strong. When the army set out on campaign, it was the 1st Battalion that went, brought up to strength with men from the 2nd Battalion. If necessary, the 2nd Battalion might follow later, but its main job was to stay at the depot in Britain, gathering and training new recruits.

A battalion was divided into ten companies, each with 40 to 80 men, a captain, two lieutenants, two sergeants, three corporals and a drummer. Eight of the ten were known as battalion companies, and two were flank companies: the grenadier and light infantry companies. The grenadiers were supposed to be the strongest and bravest men in the battalion and they were used for particularly dangerous duties. They wore white plumes and grenade badges. The light infantry were supposed to be the most agile and intelligent men and were used for skirmishing. They wore green plumes and hunting horn badges.

Because the redcoat's musket in this period was inaccurate except at very short range, men could only fight effectively if they were drawn up in tightly packed ranks. It was very important for them to practice marching and handling their guns in precise formations, obeying the word of command without delay. So most of the recruit's first months in the army were spent learning these drills on the parade ground – until he was sick of the sergeant's bellowing voice!

▷ For drill the redcoat wore a simple white jacket, with his regiment's identifying facing color on the collar and cuffs. A stiff leather neckstrap or stock kept his chin up. Sergeants took charge of his training: officers had little to do with their men until they went on campaign. Officers bought their ranks for cash.

Battalion drawn up in line

FRONT

LIGHT COMPANY

BATTALION COMPANIES

GRENADIER COMPANY

8 7 6 5 4 3 2 1

Barrack life

The redcoats were usually country-bred, aged anything between fifteen and thirty-five. They were mostly about 5 ft 7 in (1.67 m) tall: short by today's standards, probably because of poor diet. They were paid weekly; but so much was held back for their food and supplies that they were lucky to have much left over – and they had to pay for laundry out of that!

While in Britain they lived in damp old stone barracks, with up to twenty men sharing a dim, airless room. There were braziers for heating and cooking and lanterns for light. Many of the soldiers smoked pipes, so the atmosphere must have been stifling and unhealthy. Since there was only cold water drawn from an outdoor pump for washing, the smell must have been overpowering.

Some married men had their wives and children with them, and babies were actually born in these rooms, surrounded by men eating, smoking, cleaning their gear, gambling, brawling, coughing and spitting. Everyone slept on dirty straw mattresses, two or even four men together in cribs – stalls on a wide wooden shelf running along the walls. It was no life for a fussy young gentleman!

▷ A barrack room in about 1800. The only privacy for women and children was a blanket hung across their crib. On the left a redcoat helps his mate dress his hair. Until 1808 this was grown long, smeared with candle grease and soap, powdered with flour, then pulled tight round a pad and tied in a pigtail. It was so tight that a man could hardly close his eyes! Soldiers naturally tried not to go through this process too often; so their heads got filthy, and most had lice and scalp diseases. As long as their uniforms were clean and bright, their officers were not concerned.

Uniform and equipment

The eighteenth-century redcoat wore a three-cornered hat and a long-tailed coat. This was a uniform designed for show rather than for convenience on the march or in battle. By the time of the Napoleonic Wars there was some improvement, and the redcoat's uniform now consisted of a leather or felt shako cap and a short jacket. On campaign he wore loose trousers over, or instead of, his knee-breeches, and "spat" gaiters to keep his shoes on in mud.

He had a caped greatcoat for bad weather, and a blanket to sleep in. But before 1813 he had no tent. If he was lucky, he found a barn in which to spend the night, but junior officers and men usually slept in the open. They either made little shelters of branches or simply rolled up in their blankets on the cold ground. No wonder that a few months' campaigning turned the "redcoat" into a "blackcoat," as stained, ragged and patched as any beggar.

His personal equipment weighed about 60 lb (30 kg) – the same as carrying an eight-year-old child about all day! The musket, and the bayonet and cartridge pouch on their shoulder belts, weighed around 20 lb (10 kg). The haversack of rations and water bottle added 8 lb (4 kg). But the worst burden was the wooden-framed, tarred canvas knapsack for spare clothes and cleaning gear, weighing about 30 lb (15 kg). The frame dug painfully into the back, and the straps squeezed the chest. On harsh summer marches men sometimes collapsed and died of exhaustion.

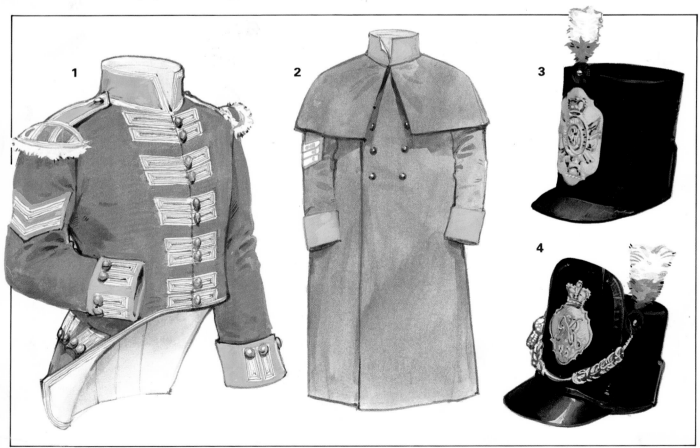

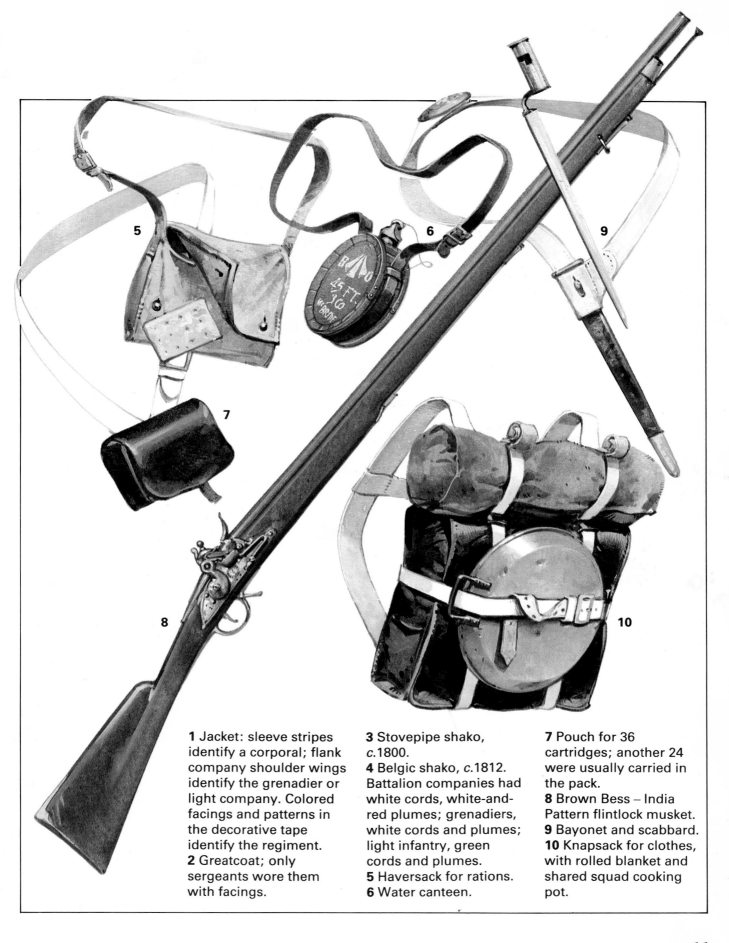

1 Jacket: sleeve stripes identify a corporal; flank company shoulder wings identify the grenadier or light company. Colored facings and patterns in the decorative tape identify the regiment.
2 Greatcoat; only sergeants wore them with facings.

3 Stovepipe shako, c.1800.
4 Belgic shako, c.1812. Battalion companies had white cords, white-and-red plumes; grenadiers, white cords and plumes; light infantry, green cords and plumes.
5 Haversack for rations.
6 Water canteen.

7 Pouch for 36 cartridges; another 24 were usually carried in the pack.
8 Brown Bess – India Pattern flintlock musket.
9 Bayonet and scabbard.
10 Knapsack for clothes, with rolled blanket and shared squad cooking pot.

Brown Bess

The redcoat's weapon, from about 1730 to 1830, was a flintlock musket nicknamed Brown Bess. (The origin of the name is not really known; it may have come from the rich brown walnut wood used to make the stock.) The Napoleonic Wars redcoat used two main patterns – the New Land and the India. They differed slightly in their fittings and length of barrel but were otherwise similar. Both were 6 ft 4 in (1.9 m) long including the bayonet and weighed about 10 lb (4.5 kg). The caliber, or width of the barrel, was .735 in (18.75 mm) – about twice the size of a modern rifle.

The musket was loaded with a paper cartridge – a tube containing a lead ball and a measured charge of gunpowder. The pictures below show the complicated method of loading and firing. Even the best soldiers could not fire more than three times a minute.

There was a pause of nearly a second between pulling the trigger and the explosion of the main charge in the barrel. The

flare of the powder in the priming pan often put the redcoat off his aim. Even under perfect conditions the Brown Bess was not accurate enough to hit an enemy at more than about 100 yd (90 m). Soldiers standing in close-packed ranks, all firing together at a tight crowd of enemy soldiers, could not do much damage at over 200 yd (180 m). It is thought that only about one shot in every 200 fired actually hit anyone.

The burning powder left a thick, clogging ash over the working parts of the gun. This had to be brushed off after a number of shots, or the musket might misfire. The flint wedge got chipped and loosened in its clamp; it had to be changed every thirty shots or so. The powder made a blinding cloud of smoke, and after a few volleys nothing could be seen more than about 50 yd (45 m) away. A long fight left the redcoat with a bruised shoulder, burned fingers and a strong thirst from biting open cartridges which left powder in his mouth. His hands and face got filthy too.

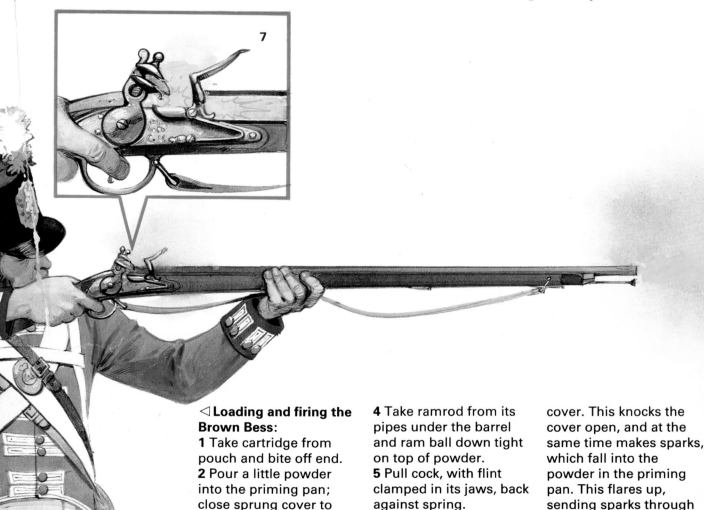

◁ **Loading and firing the Brown Bess:**
1 Take cartridge from pouch and bite off end.
2 Pour a little powder into the priming pan; close sprung cover to keep it in place.
3 Pour rest of powder, ball and paper down the muzzle of the musket.
4 Take ramrod from its pipes under the barrel and ram ball down tight on top of powder.
5 Pull cock, with flint clamped in its jaws, back against spring.
6, 7 Pull trigger: the cock falls and the flint strikes the steel plate angled upward from the pan cover. This knocks the cover open, and at the same time makes sparks, which fall into the powder in the priming pan. This flares up, sending sparks through the touch hole in the side of the barrel, setting off the main powder charge inside.

The cruel roads

The redcoat usually saw his first battle during the Peninsular War in Spain and Portugal, 1808–14; and it was there that he first made his new reputation.

During those years the Duke of Wellington led a small British army against much stronger French forces. Always outnumbered, he had to keep his troops constantly on the move. So his redcoats spent far more time marching than actually fighting.

They were expected to walk at least 15 miles (24 km) a day: less than the ancient Roman legionaries – but then the Romans had fine paved roads, while the redcoats trudged through deep mud in winter, and dust in summer! In emergencies they covered huge distances. One force marched 66 miles (105 km) in just 30 hours. In the May–December campaign season one year the Coldstream Guards marched a total of 1,700 miles (2,720 km). More often than not, the redcoat bore these cruel marches with endurance and obedience.

He showed the same dogged bravery in battle, once he learned to trust his leaders.

Wellington could not afford to lose many men, so he carefully picked the time and place for his battles. He nearly always led his redcoats to victory. He took care of their training, supplies, welfare, and the behavior of their officers as best he could. The more confident they became, the more victories they won for him.

It was a hard core of Peninsular War veterans who saved the day for Wellington at his final great battle of Waterloo in Belgium in 1815, where they stood their ground under terrible day-long attacks.

▽ British troops retreat over rough Spanish roads in winter. Under such bad conditions, even strictly disciplined regiments sometimes broke down into mobs of sullen stragglers. The rather primitive supply arrangements failed, leaving the men starving. Uniforms and boots, often of poor quality and supplied by dishonest businessmen, would fall apart on a hard march, so the redcoat had to hobble barefoot and wrapped in rags.

On the right green-clad men of the 95th Rifles move to set up a rearguard defense to keep the pursuing French cavalry at bay. This crack regiment had rifles – guns with a spiral groove inside the barrel which made the ball spin in flight, keeping it straight for about 300 yd (275 m). They were trained to fight as individuals, rather than in ranks.

Women at war

Six redcoats in each company, drawn by lot, were allowed to take their wives with them on campaign. These brave women shared all the hardship and danger of war. They helped carry their husbands' gear, nursed them if they fell sick and tried to make camp life a little more comfortable. Some became famous, like Bridget Skiddy of the 34th Foot. She used to drive officers wild by barging her way through the column of march, determined to have a "drop of hot tea" brewed ready for her Dan when he stopped each evening! If the husband was killed, such women often married another redcoat very quickly. Sergeant Dunn of the 68th Foot left his wife widowed for the fifth time when he fell at the battle of Salamanca in 1812 – within a week she was Mrs Sergeant Hubbs.

Any officer's wife could accompany her husband if she wished. She had to make all her own arrangements, however. Young girls from sheltered homes showed great bravery and resource, traveling across a war-torn country. And what began as an exciting, romantic adventure soon turned into a nightmare if they had to search among the dead and dying on the battlefield for their missing husbands.

▷ An officer and his wife ride in to a summer campground: life on campaign was not *always* miserable! They are followed by their baggage mules and a driver and maid hired in Portugal.

Before tents were issued in 1813, the redcoats took every chance to rig up shelters out of branches or sheets of canvas. When the army rested for a few days, soldiers' wives made a few extra pennies by washing, sewing and cooking for the other men.

Disciplined by the whip

Of necessity, discipline was harsh in the old army of the redcoats. For even quite small offenses a man might receive a hundred lashes from the cruel cat-o'-nine-tails. Soldiers sometimes died from their injuries after a flogging.

The officers, particularly the colonel of a battalion, could make their men's lives a misery or quite tolerable. Some were tyrants; others were kind and decent, and never ordered a flogging if they could avoid it. General Sir John Moore won many admirers for his methods of teaching men to be good soldiers by praise, reward and good example. Some of the finest regiments had the most humane commanders, like Colonel Colborne of the 52nd Light Infantry and Colonel Beckwith of the 95th Rifles.

Though flogging seems horribly cruel to us, it is true that many redcoats were very "hard cases," who did not respect kinder methods. Some boasted of being able to suffer hundreds of lashes in silence. But most soldiers gave respect and loyalty to officers who led by example, not by fear. Their writings show that they did not resent an officer's great privileges as long as he was fair and civil — and, above all, led them bravely in battle. A cowardly officer endangered their lives more than a brave one.

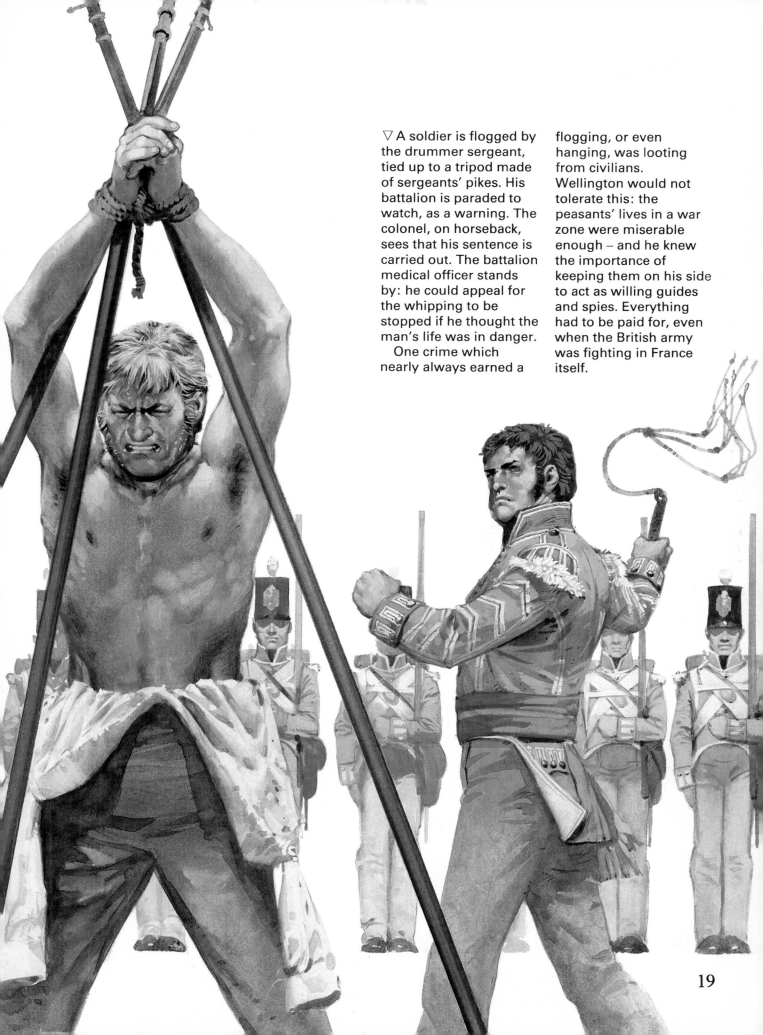

▽ A soldier is flogged by the drummer sergeant, tied up to a tripod made of sergeants' pikes. His battalion is paraded to watch, as a warning. The colonel, on horseback, sees that his sentence is carried out. The battalion medical officer stands by: he could appeal for the whipping to be stopped if he thought the man's life was in danger.

One crime which nearly always earned a flogging, or even hanging, was looting from civilians. Wellington would not tolerate this: the peasants' lives in a war zone were miserable enough – and he knew the importance of keeping them on his side to act as willing guides and spies. Everything had to be paid for, even when the British army was fighting in France itself.

The battle line

Obstinate by nature, British soldiers have usually fought better as defenders than as attackers. The redcoats won many of their victories by stubbornly standing their ground until the enemy fell back.

Battle tactics were not very complicated. Generals naturally tried to take the enemy by surprise and arranged their men in the best formations to meet enemy infantry, cavalry and cannon. Wellington always tried to place his men just behind a ridge or hilltop to save them from cannon fire until the last moment. But once they were face to face, the soldiers simply had to keep on fighting at close range until one side lost so many men that they had to retreat. Officers and sergeants had little to do but keep the ranks straight, shout the orders for loading and firing, and set an example of calmness under fire. Since there was bravery on both sides, losses were terribly high: at Waterloo Wellington lost 15,000 men out of 68,000.

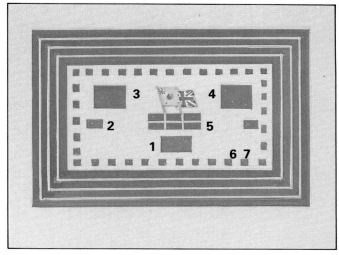

△ Battles were won by the side which chose the right formation for the particular job it had to do. A hollow square was the best defense against cavalry attack, with perhaps 150 or 200 muskets and bayonets on each side. In the middle stood the colonel and his staff (**1**); majors (**2**); band, acting as stretcher-bearers (**3**); pioneers (**4**); and the color party (**5**) – the officers with the battalion's two flags, guarded by sergeants with pikes. Junior officers (**6**) and sergeants (**7**) stood behind the rear ranks of each company.

▽ French infantry usually attacked in dense columns, so the redcoats met them drawn up in two ranks. Light infantry of both sides skirmished between the armies. When the main forces clashed, all the redcoats could fire at once. The French presented a large target at which to aim, while only the front and outside men in their column could use their muskets at any one time.

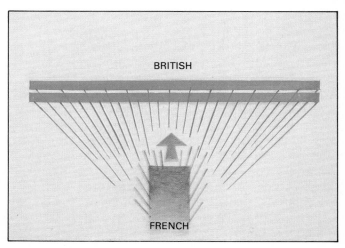

BRITISH

FRENCH

The Emperor's grenadiers

The French soldiers whom the redcoats met in battle were not volunteers but conscripts. This meant that they were forced by law to serve in the army. Some may have felt this was unjust, but their letters and diaries show that they soon got over this. They were proud to follow their brilliant soldier-emperor, who led them to many victories over Italians, Germans, Austrians, Russians and other nations.

Napoleon and his generals and marshals were men of quite humble birth. In the French army brave and intelligent men were promoted quickly, whatever their background. So senior commanders were usually younger and smarter than their equivalents in the British army. The soldiers they led were confident, loyal and experienced – and they had the "habit of victory," which is important for a soldier.

Napoleon himself hardly fought at all in Spain: he left that campaign to his generals, while he fought in eastern Europe and made his disastrous attack on Russia. So it was not until Waterloo in 1815 that Napoleon actually met the Duke of Wellington and his redcoats in battle. He had beaten so many enemies that he did not take the British army seriously. His generals who had fought in the Peninsula, and who knew how clever Wellington was at picking his ground to suit the strengths of his redcoats, warned Napoleon that he was wrong. The outcome of Waterloo proved them the better judges.

▷ French infantry charge into the attack. Infantry battalions were organized in much the same way as their British equivalents. But to give extra weight to an attack, the French sometimes grouped together the grenadiers of several battalions to form whole units of these crack troops. The uniforms of French grenadiers bore red decorations, including fringed epaulettes. Before 1813 they wore tall bearskin caps; after this date they wore shakos with red braid decorations, plumes and cords. Napoleon presented each regiment with an Eagle standard; the flag on the staff was wrapped around and covered with oilskin to protect it in battle. The standard-bearer and his NCO guards were picked for their long service and bravery. The NCOs carried pikes and pistols.

Horse, foot and guns

The redcoats of the line infantry formed the main bulk of Wellington's British troops in the Peninsula and at Waterloo. But success also depended on a well-balanced mixture of other types of troops to do different jobs during a campaign.

The redcoats were slow; they were only taught how to fight all together, waiting for orders which were carried out without question. To scout out the land and the enemy, armies needed light infantry and riflemen – fast-moving, agile troops taught to use their own initiative. There were whole units of these crack troops, apart from the light infantry company of each line battalion.

The same sort of job, but over longer distances and at greater speed, was also done by the light cavalry – the dragoons and hussars. They could also carry out surprise attacks from unexpected directions and pursue a beaten enemy, turning retreat into

flight. Heavy cavalry were used in solid masses on the battlefield to deliver thundering charges at enemy infantry already shaken by infantry or cannon fire.

The artillery's cannons were divided between horse and foot batteries. The light, fast horse artillery could advance with the cavalry, supporting their charges with close-up fire. The heavier foot artillery fired from fixed positions and usually stayed in one place throughout a battle.

▽ Riflemen, light dragoon, foot artilleryman and light infantry officer, relaxing around a cooking fire. The day's ration was 1 lb ($\frac{1}{2}$ kg) of beef; about the same of bread or hard biscuit; 1 pt ($\frac{1}{2}$ liter) of wine, or a third that amount of gin or rum. Fresh food was bought, if available, from nearby farmers. The supply of beef was usually reliable: cattle marched with the army, and about 300 were slaughtered each night. Bread arrived less frequently and when it did it was stale, moldy and maggoty. An inch-thick biscuit in the breast pocket of Lieutenant Madden, 43rd Foot, was hard enough to save his life: a French musket ball smashed it, but was turned away from his heart in the process!

Riflemen wore green. Light cavalry wore blue tunics and special shakos or fur busbies. Foot artillery wore blue tunics, but otherwise looked like redcoat infantry. Officers of the crack light infantry copied some elements of cavalry uniforms.

Siege and storm

Apart from battles in open country, there were many sieges in the Napoleonic Wars. If troops found their way blocked by a fortress with cannons on the walls, they could not advance until they had captured it. Few roads were suitable for carrying an army's wagons and cannons, so there was little choice of route.

Sieges were the redcoat's worst ordeal, costing hundreds of lives from sickness and wounds. An army that camped in one place for many weeks was often swept by disease. The redcoats had to dig trenches closer and closer to the walls, under constant fire from the defenders. Meanwhile the artillery tried to pound gaps in the walls to allow the infantry to climb up with ladders and fight their way through into the town.

The defending garrison was always offered a chance to surrender once the gap in the wall was big enough for storming. Storming cost so many lives that it was avoided if possible. Throughout history it was the grim custom that defenders who forced attackers to actually fight their way in were killed without mercy, rather than being taken prisoner. This was because the stormers suffered so terribly. They had to scramble over beams studded with sharp blades, under a shower of bombs and fire-pots. And of course, the defenders of a gap in the wall knew just where to wait with guns loaded and ready. Surviving attackers, even if they were usually well-disciplined troops, often carried out murderous massacres when the town finally fell.

▷ Scottish Highland infantry of Wellington's army storm a French-held town in the Peninsula. Highland battalions, such as the Black Watch and the Gordons, went on to fight very bravely at Waterloo in 1815. They had the reputation of being sober, religious, well-behaved men in camp, but fearsome fighters in battle. They wore uniforms combining the redcoat's jacket with their traditional kilt, and bonnet.

In the background other soldiers struggle up the scaling ladders while the defenders shoot at them and throw heavy stones. The bearded man with an axe is a pioneer: each battalion had a squad of these men. They did heavy work such as cutting paths through woodland, building defenses, and – as here – tearing down enemy barricades.

The fate of the wounded

Big, soft lead bullets, swords and lances made terrible wounds. The doctors who attended the wounded were hopelessly overworked. Each battalion had only one surgeon and two assistants, and in a single big battle they might easily have 200 or 300 wounded men to care for.

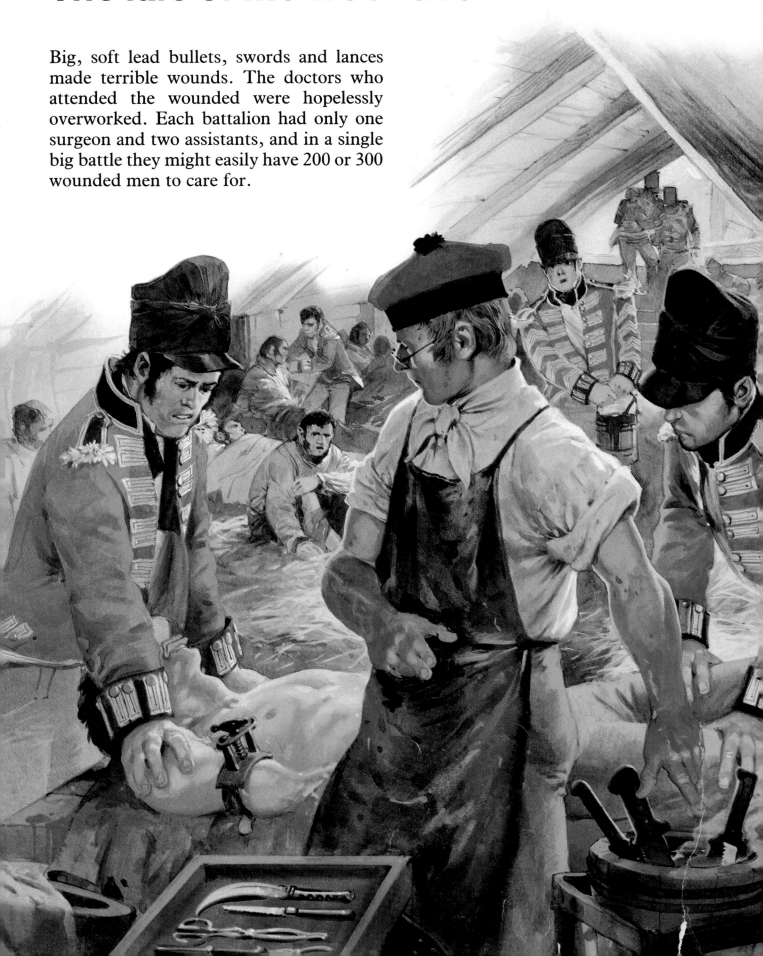

Doctors in those days knew little of the causes of infection. They operated on the wounded in filthy conditions, in any handy cottage, barn or stable. Since most wounds became infected anyway, they almost always cut off a wounded arm or leg. Because there were no drugs to put the patient to sleep, he had to endure the operation wide awake, with only a stiff drink and a gag to bite on in his agony. But it is extraordinary to read how many men suffered this nightmare in silence, without even being held down.

Private Shadrack Byfield, whose arm was amputated, wrote: "The operation was tedious and painful, but I was enabled to bear it pretty well . . . The stump of my arm soon healed, and three days after I was able to play a game of Fives [a vigorous team ball game] for a quart of rum . . ."

Despite the danger of wounds in close-range battles, it was in fact disease which killed most unlucky redcoats. A British force fighting around Walcheren in the Low Countries in 1809 lost 106 men in battle, but 4,000 died from disease. A further 10,000 men survived the sickness, but were more or less invalids for the rest of their lives. In the Peninsular War 800 men, out of a total strength of 2,000 in the 1st Foot Guards, died of fever in the first five months of 1813. If surgeons' first aid posts were dreadful, base hospitals were even worse. To be sent to hospital was little better than a death sentence, and sick men died there in their thousands.

◁ A surgeon operates on a wounded redcoat. Although the men were very brave, they often died of shock from the pain of a long, agonizing operation. It is likely that as many as one in three died after treatment. Even so, some amazing recoveries were recorded. A redcoat who fought in the storming of Badajoz in Spain, where 5,000 redcoats fell, survived 13 bayonet wounds.

▷ Recovery was not the end of a wounded man's misery, however. Very few were given a pension, and even the lucky ones got only a few pennies a day. Many a brave soldier who had worn the red coat in battle continued to wear it as a starving beggar for the rest of his life.

Glossary

Battery An artillery unit, usually with six cannons; or, the position of a number of cannons on the battlefield.

Brown Bess Soldiers' nickname for the flintlock musket used from about 1730 to 1830 by the British redcoat.

Busby Cylindrical fur cap worn by some light cavalry regiments.

Canteen Bottle or small keg used by soldiers for carrying drinking water.

Captain Junior officer in the army, in command of a company of about 80 men.

Cartridge Paper tube holding the ball and powder for one loading of a musket.

Company Small military unit of about 80 men at full strength, but often much smaller when weakened by casualties. Ten companies made up a battalion.

Corporal Senior soldier; there were three to each company in the British army of the Napoleonic Wars.

Dragoon Type of cavalry soldier; originally a soldier trained and equipped to fight either on horseback or on foot, but by 1800 an ordinary light horseman.

Facings Areas of colored cloth on the collar, cuffs and shoulder straps of a redcoat's jacket which helped identify the regiment at a glance.

Grenadier company The senior company in an infantry battalion, often made up of the biggest, strongest, bravest men. Originally, in the late 1600s and early 1700s, they were picked to advance ahead of the other redcoats and throw hand grenades. By the Napoleonic Wars grenades were rarely used, but the name stuck.

Hussar Type of light cavalry soldier.

Lieutenant Junior officer in the army; two served in each company of about 80 men, under command of a captain.

Light infantry Foot soldiers trained to fight as skirmishers, away from the main body of troops. There were several regiments of redcoat light infantry in Wellington's army, apart from the light company in each line battalion.

NCO Non-commissioned officer – the term for sergeants and corporals.

Press-gang Party of sailors under command of an officer sent ashore to kidnap men for forced service in the Royal Navy.

Priming The small amount of gunpowder poured into the priming pan on the side of a musket's firing mechanism. The spark from the flint set it on fire, and the priming set off the main charge.

Sergeant Senior soldier; there were two to each company in the British army of this period.

Shako Tall, cylindrical military cap with a peak over the eyes; made of felt or leather, it was decorated with a badge, braided cords and/or colored tufts and plumes.

Skirmishers Men who fought in loose groups or individually, using their own initiative and taking advantage of cover, rather than standing in mass formations and all firing together on the command.

Stock The wooden part of a musket; also, a leather neckband worn with the redcoat's uniform to keep his chin up.

Surgeon In this period most military doctors were called surgeons, even though they were responsible for prescribing medicine as well as performing operations.

Timechart

These are the dates of the redcoat's main campaigns; great events were happening at the same time in Germany, Austria and Russia, which occupied much of Napoleon's attention.

1808 General Sir Arthur Wellesley leads a small British army to Portugal to help Spain and Portugal against their French occupiers. After he wins battles at Rolica and Vimiero there is a political row, and Wellesley is recalled to England. He is replaced by Sir John Moore.

January 1809 Moore's army is forced into a miserable winter retreat to Corunna, where Moore is killed. Wellesley returns to Portugal to take command in April. He advances rapidly, driving the French out of Portugal. (By this time Napoleon had left the campaign to his subordinates.)

July 1809 Wellesley's army beats the French at Talavera, and he is made Viscount Wellington.

September 1810 The French Marshal Masséna, invading Portugal from Spain once more, is beaten at Bussaco. Wellington's redcoats pull back into comfortable defenses, prepared long beforehand, and sit out the winter around Torres Vedras near Lisbon. Outside, the French starve – and finally retreat.

May 1811 Wellington beats Masséna, with difficulty, at Fuentes d'Onoro in Spain. Meanwhile, part of his army under General Beresford is horribly cut up at Albuera – the redcoat's costliest victory.

Winter 1811–12 Wellington takes Cuidad Rodrigo and Badajoz, vital fortresses on the Portuguese-Spanish border. After heavy losses on the walls of Badajoz, redcoats, drunk on looted wine, cruelly sack the town. Wellington advances into Spain again and beats another French army at Salamanca in July 1812.

Winter 1812–13 Wellington's siege of Burgos fails, and he is forced to retreat with his hungry and sullen army. (But meanwhile, in Russia, Napoleon's Grand Army is losing no less than 300,000 men in the terrible retreat from Moscow.)

1813 Heartened by Napoleon's defeat in Russia, Austria, Germany and other countries rise up to fight the French. Napoleon is brilliantly successful at raising a new army and defending his territory in Germany. Meanwhile, Wellington advances through Spain. He beats the French at Vittoria in June; and the next winter finds the redcoats fighting in the Pyrenees.

Spring 1814 While Napoleon resists invasion by the eastern European allies, Wellington advances into France from the south, and in April takes Toulouse. Meanwhile, Paris falls to the eastern allies. On April 11 Napoleon gives up his throne and goes into exile on the island of Elba.

March 1, 1815 Napoleon escapes from Elba and returns to France. His old soldiers flock to join him. In June he makes a sudden advance into Belgium.

June 16–18, 1815 Surprised by Napoleon's advance, the Prussian General Blücher is roughly handled at Ligny; and Wellington only just escapes defeat by Marshal Ney at Quatre Bras. But both armies retreat in good order; and at Waterloo on June 18 Wellington's redcoats fend off terrible French attacks all day. In the evening Blücher's Prussians arrive at last, and the French are routed. Napoleon is sent into exile for life on the island of St Helena.

Index

PRINTED IN BELGIUM BY
proost
INTERNATIONAL BOOK PRODUCTION